Lost in Transition

poems by

Sandra Kolankiewicz

Finishing Line Press
Georgetown, Kentucky

Lost in Transition

Copyright © 2017 by Sandra Kolankiewicz
ISBN 978-1-63534-187-4 First Edition
All rights reserved under International and Pan-American Copyright Conventions.
No part of this book may be reproduced in any manner whatsoever without written permission from the publisher, except in the case of brief quotations embodied in critical articles and reviews.

ACKNOWLEDGMENTS

"Love Poem," *Forge Journal*
"As Long As We Both," "Visitation," *SNReview*
"The Question Is," *Inertia*
"Earthly Blessings," *The Bellingham Review*
"My Mental Illness," *The Analectic*, pending
"Getting Rid of the Cat," *Citron Review*
"Love Child," "Sewing," *Psychic Meatloaf*
"When I Was Sick, She Said," *WomenArts Quarterly*
"Stimulus," *Shark Reef*
"The Woman in the Glass," *Colorado North Review*
"Sister," *Confrontation*
"February 1861," "Poem for the Lost Silver Ring," *First Literary Review East*
 "Sidewise Apology," *Rhino*
"The Lungfish," *Meat for Tea*
"At the Home for Delinquent Poems," *Curbside Splendor*
"Neighborhood Watch," *Storm Cellar*
"Lost in Transition," *Transnational Review*
"After the Funeral," "Mind Game," *The Voices Project*
 "In Between Layoffs," "User's Lament," *Argilo*, Gival Press
"In Case You Forgot," "Instead of Convertible," "Which is a Universe," *Black Fox*

Publisher: Leah Maines

Editor: Christen Kincaid

Cover Art: Sandra Kolankiewicz

Author Photo: Sandra Kolankiewicz

Cover Design: Elizabeth Maines McCleavy

Printed in the USA on acid-free paper.
Order online: www.finishinglinepress.com
 also available on amazon.com

Author inquiries and mail orders:
Finishing Line Press
P. O. Box 1626
Georgetown, Kentucky 40324
U. S. A.

Table of Contents

Love Poem 1
Visitation 2
As Long As We Both 3
The Question Is 4
Earthly Blessings 5
My Mental Illness 6
Getting Rid of the Cat 8
Sewing 9
Love Child 10
When I Was Sick, She Said 11
Stimulus 12
Sister 13
For the Lost Silver Ring 14
February 1861 15
Sidewise Apology 16
The Lungfish 17
At the Home for Delinquent Poems 18
Neighborhood Watch 19
Lost in Transition 20
Mind Game 21
After the Funeral 22
User's Lament 23
In Between Layoffs 24
In Case You Forgot 25
Instead of Convertible 26
Which Is a Universe 27

For Cheryl Cesta and our enduring friendship.

Love Poem

I regret I do not have a love whose wrinkles I watch increase.

Instead, I accept the usual convention
because someone is
depending on me.

Instead, I study my own creeping lines,
the furrows from nose to chin,
upward scratches on the lip,
the creeping jowl—
the face emerging, a beloved,
familiar potato crumpling.

A Visitation

First they should have told me what killed
them. Why should I have to ask? There
they were at the foot of my bed when I
awoke: that fancy dress, that expensive tie
with horse bridles. *Our baby's back,* I
whispered though he'd been gone for years.
We'd heard she married, always wondered
who could have caught our bird and
speculated the way some people watched
Jeopardy. Was it when I spanked her
outside of church? That time she wanted to
see the movies? Was she angry because he
was always working? Maybe we gave her
too much of one thing and not enough of
another, now there in her Chanel suit, hair
cropped, looking as if she were alive when
I closed my eyes, pretended to be asleep.

As Long As We Both

We begin by saying
everything will be different
when those bells toll whose I am,
whose you are.

Neither may live and lie.

A girl falls off the roof,
the boys pitch eggs at cars, throw zucchini,
finally bottles at the house across the street
while you and I are swearing
we will rise above
all this.

The Question Is

who would I call now? The men all have
bellies, hair going, gone, or suspicious. Call,
just to chat. To someone who isn't a woman
because women chat. Women chat all the

time. Because that thing doesn't happen
to me anymore. I can have just a conversation
now, don't bring up a past or a future, just
the mediocrity of the daily, never

mention that one time in July on that inner tube,
that one summer, that one afternoon, you in
your sleeveless shirt as we left our dates
speechless on the sand while we just floated

away from them and never returned. What
did they say to each other? We went with the
current, the Marlboros and matches somehow
still dry, which made us giddy though we

drifted further and further, bobbing off, never
mentioning the ones on the beach watching
us smoking and laughing, growing smaller
and smaller, until finally we were gone.

Earthly Blessings

For a while it worked. Then they began to hurt us: the blessings we bore from meeting to meeting, always sheepishly greeting each other as we went room to room, house to house, public space to public space. We hefted on our backs when our arms were too tired, on days the weight went limp on purpose, and we'd have to drag it behind, leaving long tracks in the sand. The ministers warned that, since we acquired them through grace, we were bound to them from this world to the next, that they were, in fact, the sole bridge to where we were going, the only way to arrive, price of the passage if we just figured the route. We asked: *how good can they be if they make us slaves instead of servants?* Better to lay them by the banks, with food if you have to, and be done, make your way by splashing upstream to avoid leaving a scent.

My Mental Illness

was what got me the job. I could
remember everything, especially the

details most would rather forget.
The time my college room mate

and her boyfriend, for instance,
so drunk during intercourse, just passed out.

When I opened her door to see why still
a candle burned so late into the night,

there they were: naked, halted mid-flail, gone slack
mid cry, oblivious to each other's

dreams as I covered them up, bent to
shield the wall from wax, blew the flame

out. That was thirty years before, recalling over
endive, I brought it up in front of a new

friend of hers, a woman I didn't know.
Two pairs of tight lips—

I saw the future: no more lunches, invitations,
presents, Saturday

morning phone calls. I had spoken what
everyone knows was unspeakable

but me, big tongue wagging
like the tail of a stupid dog

who does not know the afternoon
is hot and will never be over.

Why the impulse to grab a
stranger by the hand to show the letter

from my cousin's husband? Where is the brake to
stop the moving train

that is the sentence speeding from my
mouth so I don't make the old lady

angry, the grocer afraid, my husband embarrassed?
But back to the details

that I never forget, the inventories
that I keep making, those reminders

that at times I even follow, which is hard.
I have to start organizing

then, must initiate talking,
negotiating, weighing,

begin the braying away of that jiggle
in my leg. I must relinquish following

behind you with the vacuum,
loitering beside you in the museum

to make sure you look correctly
at the light escaping Van Gogh's tired eyes

with their vanquished, bandaged ear—
as if only I can see the green that's in

them—as if somehow I should know
what to reveal and when to hide—

as though I had any choice in the matter, didn't
wish I could just forget it all.

Getting Rid of the Cat

We all missed her afterwards, even my dad
though she once pissed in his shoes. That was after the baby.
The cat was angry, just like my Memaw who never
visited again after the first time though when she
was here the cat slept wrapped around her head with
pillows. Every morning for a week we tip toed
beside the extra mattress in the living room till she
woke and smoked. *'Don't talk to me until I've had a
Marlboro,'* she said. After the cat jumped into the
crib a third time, so much wet yellow spreading out
to the edge of the sheet, as if she'd been saving it,
my dad drove out in the county to toss her at a dairy
farm. Still, my mother kept looking out the back
door when it snowed, especially after my brother got
sick. She cranked and cranked that swinging seat or
paced the halls with him while he wailed. Every day
we listened to that sound he made, like a whining
rock she carried room to room, until the snow rose
above the roof, turned to rain, and he was gone.

Sewing

The point of it, the eye of the needle
slides in and through, up
and through again.
Colors change,

the yarn thickens, weakens,
does not break.
The pattern lingers in the thread,
waits in the hand.

Fine meals, hard falls from horses,
whole and parts of oranges,
Christmas seals, honey labels.
The other hand cradles the next color.

Love Child

The flowers in the vase first wilted,
then dried to brittle flakes swept
across the linoleum floor. Dusk is

weeping. The bells in the church
down the street ring five times.
My fingers tap the notes of the hours,

the long day dangling from my wrist,
the sleeping baby tucked beneath my
brown arm. The sky is white. A

pocket watch ticks on the dresser.
Two hundred miles beyond the door,
you aim a pistol at a rusted can.

When I was Sick, She Said

When I was sick, she said,
I would imagine that I crawled here to die.

She squatted, leaning back in her hiking boots,
elbows resting on her knees, fingers
tearing a brown leaf along its arteries.

He looked around the cave, not knowing
whether he should laugh.
The snow outside was fresh, only
their footprints coming in.
The falls were frozen, milky blue-green.
Somewhere inside the column of ice
he could hear water running.

Stimulus

Soon I was coveting again: latest
Kenmore refrigerator, a larger
hot tub, fresh paper for the powder room.
All night I wanted upgrades: stove, glasses,
dryer, computer, satellite channels,
husband. The children slept snug in their beds,
stuck on Christmas, riding the eternal
Dreamland Express to the midnight discount
store. One day, the girl up the block parked a
bright Soul, dull Ford gone from her drive. Someone
in back installed a slate roof. Our brick streets
yielded as men in brand new reflective
vests rolled down clean tar. We didn't care that
the routes were lined with cones, one-lane all the
way to the mall, just as long as asphalt
got things moving here. By then, families
with signs had gone back to Florida, the
food banks restocked with boxed macaroni.

Sister

Our mother, the rose-printed quilt on her lap,
never looks at you, never sees
the makeup, the rolled up skirt,
the dirty legs.

You crawl into bed, whisper across the room
the strange things he want to do,
his breath over your breasts,
the way he pleaded.
I can almost see your eyes,
their glint of power in the dark,
how they shine from the face
of such a young girl.

For the Lost Silver Ring

She's oiled and baking in the sun when a song
leaps out at her from the radio— or perhaps
she's fallen asleep, dreaming it over and over
as if scrubbing a dirty corner, the years
running themselves round and round, melting
like tigers to butter— before the white lace
dress, the black ties, the wrapped presents
stacked on a table in a corner— before the
service, the turning page, the empty rooms—
arguing with him in an alley, weaving back
and forth, accusing what she still cannot
remember—even now.

February 1861

The air is so dried in the furnace-heated tenements that, after leaving the factory with their mothers, the children commonly light the lamps at home with their fingertips, dragging their socks on the carpets, bodies so charged with electric fluid that when they raise their fingers toward a burner, a spark jumps forth adequate enough to ignite the gas.

Sidewise Apology

Look, Fred, it's not your head. It's mine. Don't bother
with the sledge hammer; another door yawns behind

this one. Stand up your bicycle and walk it home before
I use my valve stem on your tires. Wrap up the change

between your sofa cushions before your quarters
disappear. Leave food out for the cat I won't feed when

I see he needs me. Wait thirty years for this bus. This
turtle will be even slower at a hundred, plenty of

barnacles, the usual *chelona* when you have lived too
long. Accept my regret covered as it is with mustard

when you prefer ketchup. Remind yourself of the hole
in my exhaust that leaks combustion so I cannot get up

to speed. Tell yourself, you might have been me had
circumstances been different and character nothing.

The Lungfish

We are star-crossed lovers who jumped into the
lake and stayed there, our lungs shrinking to
gills now too atrophied to breathe so we survive
the seasonal drought by burrowing into the mud,
estivating through the dry season. Hidden deep
below the mussels and the clams, settled among
the sludge and stones, we slow our metabolism,
convert protein from ammonia to urea so we
never age. Instead, we wait, sometimes for
years, without dreaming, anticipate the rains and
the moment we will flex and rise, leave the
water to lunge onto land, chase frogs in the
grass, shifting one fin forward, then another,
both front and back, as if they were hands and
feet. Though denied our ancestry, we are true
carnivores. Even snakes are tetrapods.

At the Home for Delinquent Poems

When they scratch at the door, I open it,
invite them in, thinking I'll fix them up,
nourish and release them, but instead of
getting well, they soon take full advantage,
sulking and lounging on my sofa, both
ignoring and sneering at me, the old stranger
in bathrobe and slippers doing their laundry
and dishes as if I'm their servant and stuck
on some old vision, loyal despite the facts.

Neighborhood Watch

Before dawn each morning I see the
obvious parts of his daily routine.
First the bedroom light flips on.
Within seconds the discreet square
that is the bath goes white, his house
the tallest, standing beside where I
sit on my small porch in the dark,
sometimes with a blanket, no longer
needing to raise eyes to know when
he moves from washing his face,
brushing his teeth, into the walk-in
closet that used to be the nursery. For
a moment all the lights go on at
once, patch of lawn between us tiled
with yellow rectangles even as the
sun begins to transition from the
other side of the world. Then he
sends the upper floor back into
what's left of night, the kitchen
ablaze behind blinds. I consider it
throughout the day, knowing all
about him but the particulars, no one
to care after he drives off in his Jeep.

Lost in Transition

The ones left stay for a reason, their health
        just as sound as the market, family

a line crossing only the y axis
        on the graph of a polynomial

function, never reaching the x, having
        little more than negative numbers when

the leading coefficient is even.
        The devil is in the lack of detail,

the clues you don't notice until you
        get the call, then wonder how you lost your

Eagle Scout. Below the skin, our walls are
        leaking, unmaking, even the organs.

We're allergic to whatever crosses
        beyond where it's meant to be, which is every

thing in a slivered world, turning on our
        selves, then settling in, repelled by others.

Mind Game

Too much sky, you said, so I shaded it,
        the firmament become the lid to a
                box without windows, dark and hot within
        like the petals of an orchid steaming
in the jungle after a rain which then
        became oppressive, a sauna with no
                door. *I preferred the jar*, you said. *At least*
    we could see. Immediately we were
surrounded by curved glass erasing the
        edges of everything on the other
                side, holes punched in the screw-on top above
    to give us air. *But there is nowhere to*
hide, you said, not wanting to be like that
        performance artist who lived in a clear
                box hung on a wall and defecated
    in public behind a towel with a
bucket. I added a kitchen matchbox
        on its side, partially opened and filled
                with crayon markings like a forgotten
    surprise. *What shall we do now*, you wondered,
that it's just us and the stagnant air, the
        world beyond out of focus, just a range
                of shifting blobs changing places, though you
    were already sitting down with open
palms, having surrendered to the image.

After the Funeral

When you lose track of where you are in space,
    the air spins, the nature of light alters.
        An unseen presence takes you under its
wing, whispers in your ear, explaining all
    about disasters is right, for like death,
        tragedy is the only reason we
pause and look at one another. I saw
    your eyes sliding among the crowd for a
        person to talk to, yet you chose no one,
instead walked through the door, the only face
    free of attachments though you probably
        felt lonely. Now, I can't see your body
but hear your voice, can't touch you but forgive
    those words you spoke, trading our secrets like
        currency in a dry economy.
I'm grateful for your protection while I
    had it, now relieved to be released from
        the habits and obligations of love.

User's Lament

I would have paid more attention, stuck on
        repeat, dissatisfied but unable

to change, all my complaints lined up to be
        handed over one by one as soon as

the cash came out. I should have removed my
        shoes, massaged my feet instead, but just for

what? Instead, I activated widgets
        in the program, let loose a worm, Malware

of desire pretending to be other
        than itself—like the rest of us—most of

my flourishes useless as a blown egg,
        fragile, worthy only of display, my

accessories outdated sooner than
        usual and earlier than the norm.

In Between Lay Offs

As a result, among other things, the
catalogue reads sketchy. Even if they
might catch a mistake, most of them
are confused between page one and ten, for
each contradicts the other. The debate
is on, starting in the boardroom, stretching
out across divisions, more than trickling
down. Today each on his own will choose to
forgo the company picnic, pronouns
not having been changed in Human
Resources in time for the fiscal year.

In Case You Forgot

Then I got to the end, and I have
        to tell you I was not at all pleased.

What they had in mind for me was not
        what I expected, and by then I

had given so much that you can just
        imagine. There wasn't enough. If

I had time just to remember what
        was missing, taken by so many.

Instead of a Convertible

You watched yourself, didn't you, slip out of
      what cloaked you, as if dissociation
came naturally, impossible to
      stop what you don't acknowledge, distance the
same as the space between you on the bed
      and you on the ceiling, someone else's
husband lying down with someone else's
      wife, no kitchen to be cleaned in the next
room, laundry done, shopping left for later.
      Forgiveness remains in the drawer with
regret, coming out on holidays with
      the silver and what's left of the bridal
porcelain after twenty-eight years. Now
      I know one can act without thinking or
feeling, impulse stronger than guilt. Faces
      can be thrust before you asking why when
you have no answer, blame as much a part
      of you as your t shirt. After fifty,
adults pretend they are not children, by
      then having circled back to what troubled
them at puberty, aware that going
      forward is the same as falling behind.

Which Is a Universe Inside

Then the moon was sinking on the other
side of the city, having spent all night
climbing, crossing, and peaking not only
to assure lovers they exist but to
give parasite eggs reason to hatch, greet
life inside a biofilm which is a
universe inside an intestine with
pathogens communicating to each
other through a grid of electrical
impulses like a city seen at night
from the stratosphere. Lying across one
another, legs not yet heavy on bone
and arms too soon to fall asleep, we watch
the steady shine go from one window to
the next, by dawn framed behind bare trees and
distant clouds, the water from our faucets
clean, the decisions we are making clear.

Over 300 of **Sandra Kolankiewicz's** poems and stories have appeared in reviews and anthologies, most recently in *New World Writing, BlazeVox, Gargoyle, Prairie Schooner, Fifth Wednesday, ArGiLo, Prick of the Spindle, Per Contra,* and *Pif. Turning Inside Out* won the 2008 fall Black River contest at Black Lawrence Press. In 2014, Finishing Line Press published *The Way You Will Go. When I Fell,* a novel with 76 color illustrations by Kathy Skerritt, is available from Web-e-Books.

She considers her subject matter to be domestic life, which is not for the faint of heart. Living a life established around the hearth, one encounters all of the joys and tragedies associated with the human experience: birth and death, success and failure, monetary struggles, the balance between work and family, and the tension between the ideal and the real. For her, poetry allows escape, redemption, compassion, and the opportunity to experience the primacy of creative energy.

www.ingramcontent.com/pod-product-compliance
Lightning Source LLC
LaVergne TN
LVHW041512070426
835507LV00012B/1522